How to Draw Awesome Vehicles

Land, Sea, and Air

BARRON'S

Created and produced by Green Android Ltd
Illustrated by Fiona Gowen

First edition for North America
published in 2015 by
Barron's Educational Series, Inc.

Copyright © Green Android Ltd 2014

Green Android Ltd
49 Beaumont Court
Upper Clapton Road
London E5 8BG
United Kingdom
www.greenandroid.co.uk

All inquiries should be addressed to:
Barron's Educational Series, Inc.
250 Wireless Boulevard
Hauppauge, NY 11788
www.barronseduc.com

ISBN: 978-1-4380-0582-9

Date of Manufacture: January 2015
Manufactured by:
Toppan Leefung Printing Co., Ltd.,
Dongguan, China

Printed in China
9 8 7 6 5 4 3 2 1

Contents

4 Huge Haulers

6 Super Racers

8 Fantastic Builders

10 Extreme Supercars

12 To the Rescue

14 Mighty Trains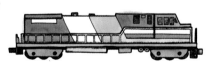

16 Groovy Bikes

18 Rugged Racers

20 Off-roaders

22 On the Water

24 Underwater Explorers

26 In the Sky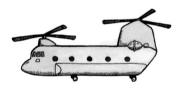

28 Aerobatic Fliers

30 Futuristic Travelers

Page 32 has an index of everything to draw in this book.

How to Draw
Huge Haulers

Big rigs are used to haul heavy freight from one place to another. Some of these trucks are so powerful they can pull several trailers at once.

HEAVY LOAD

STOP

1 Start your picture by drawing the truck's three large wheels.

2 You can now draw the base and wheel arch of the truck. Add a rectangle for the fuel tank.

3 Now draw an outline for the cab and the exhaust pipe.

 Add the driver's window to the cab and some windows to the above-cab sleeping compartment.

 Add some detail to your drawing, such as air inlets on the bonnet and panels on the side of the cab.

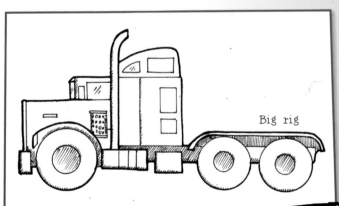

Big rig

To finish your drawing, add some shading to the areas of the truck that are in shadow.

More to Draw

Trucks come in many shapes and sizes. They are all designed to carry specific types of loads.

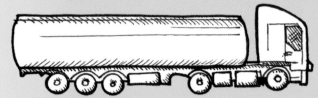

Fuel tanker

Car transporter

Concrete mixer

Lowboy

Dump truck

Road train

Delivery truck

Log transporter

WIDE VEHICLE

Garbage truck

How to Draw

Super Racers

Nothing beats the noise and excitement of a race track. Formula One racing is a fast and dangerous motor sport. Drivers need nerves of steel!

1 Start your race car picture by drawing a pair of wheels.

2 Draw two parallel lines connecting the two wheels. This is the base of your car.

3 Now draw the outline of the race car between the two wheels.

More to Draw
Racing vehicles come in all shapes and sizes,
from the smallest kart to enormous racing trucks.

Street racer

Dragster

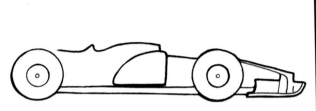

4 Draw the long, thin bonnet of the race car onto the front of the right-hand wheel.

Stock car

Off-road racer

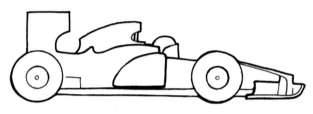

5 Now you can add the helmet of the driver, the engine intake behind the driver, and the large rear wing.

Speedway racer

Formula One car

Rally car

Truck racer

6 To finish the drawing, go over the lines and add some shading. This will help give it a realistic look.

Superkart

Endurance racer

How to Draw
Fantastic Builders

Construction sites are amazing places where machines haul, dig, and lift materials. This roller is used to flatten the ground when making roads.

1 Draw a rear wheel with a rectangle through it and a smaller back wheel.

2 You can now join the two wheels together by drawing the base of the cab.

3 Draw the cab onto the base. Add windows for the driver to see through.

4 Draw the engine cover and exhaust pipe onto the back of the roller.

Backhoe loader

More to Draw

Here are some more working vehicles that you could add to drawings of construction sites.

Bulldozer

Telehandler

5 Add the side mirror and some lights. Add details to the roller's body, such as rivets and panels.

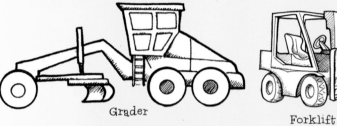

Grader

Forklift

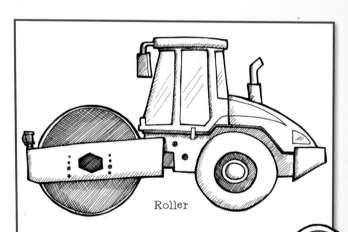

Roller

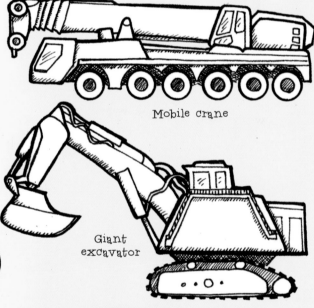

Mobile crane

Giant excavator

6 Finish your drawing of a roller by shading some areas and adding lines for reflections onto the windows.

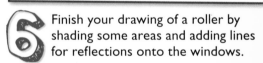

Mini excavator

Giant dump truck

Extreme Supercars

Supercars are some of the fastest and most stylish cars. These exotic cars offer incredible performance on the road or on the race track.

START

1 Start your supercar drawing with two circles for the wheels.

2 Now you can draw the outline of the supercar around the two wheels.

3 Add the car's window, door, and wheel arch to the drawing.

Gumpert Apollo

Koenigsegg Agera R

4 Add details for the lights, mirror, seat, door handle, and air intakes on the side of the car.

5 Add a small circle at each wheel's center, then add the spokes.

Bugatti Veyron SS

6 Finish your drawing by going over the main lines again, and then add some shading to the car.

Lamborghini Aventador LP700

McLaren F1

Saleen S7

How to Draw

To the Rescue

Rescue vehicles are amazing machines that help the rescue teams perform life-saving jobs as quickly and safely as possible.

1 Start your drawing with the outline of the ladder.

2 You can now add the outline of the fire engine underneath the ladder.

3 Draw shapes connecting the engine to the ladder, then add a bumper and wheels.

4 Draw the details for the ladder, and then add the apparatus and dials onto the engine.

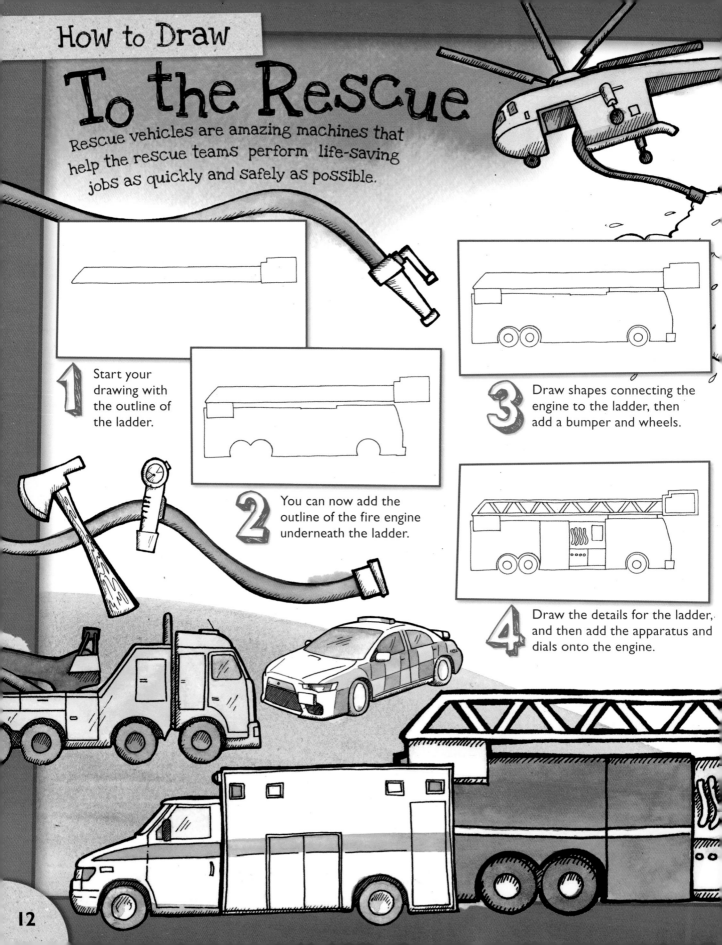

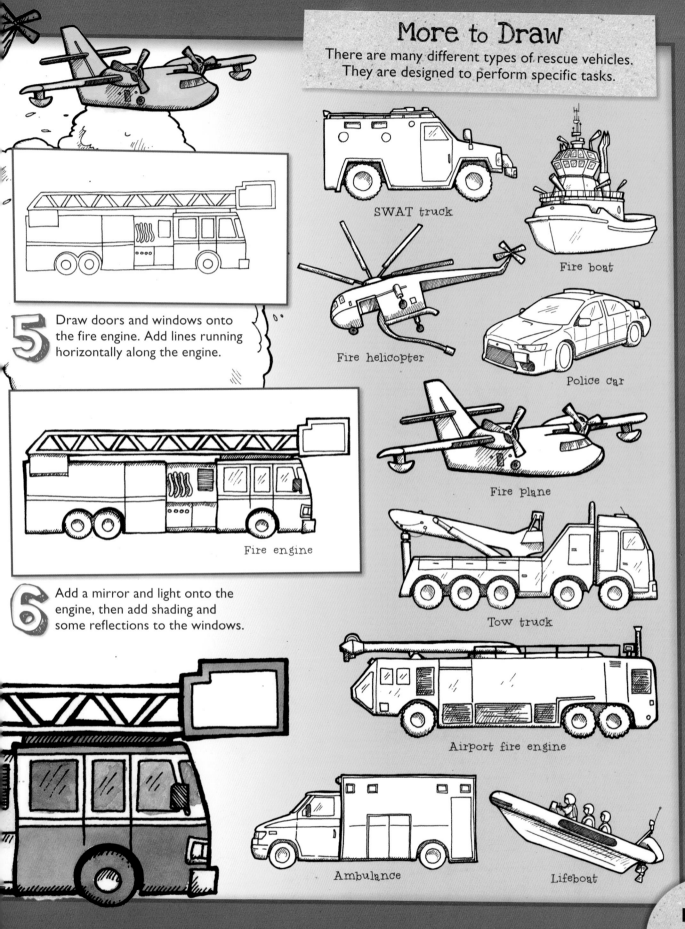

There are many different types of rescue vehicles.
They are designed to perform specific tasks.

SWAT truck

Fire boat

5 Draw doors and windows onto the fire engine. Add lines running horizontally along the engine.

Fire helicopter

Police car

Fire engine

Fire plane

6 Add a mirror and light onto the engine, then add shading and some reflections to the windows.

Tow truck

Airport fire engine

Ambulance

Lifeboat

13

How to Draw
Mighty Trains

Railroads were built all over the world to carry people and goods. Trains have evolved from early steam-powered engines to high-speed bullet trains.

Double decker train

1 Draw the thin base and the outline of the train engine.

2 You can now add two sets of wheels underneath the base of the train.

3 Draw lines inside the train to separate the different sections of the train.

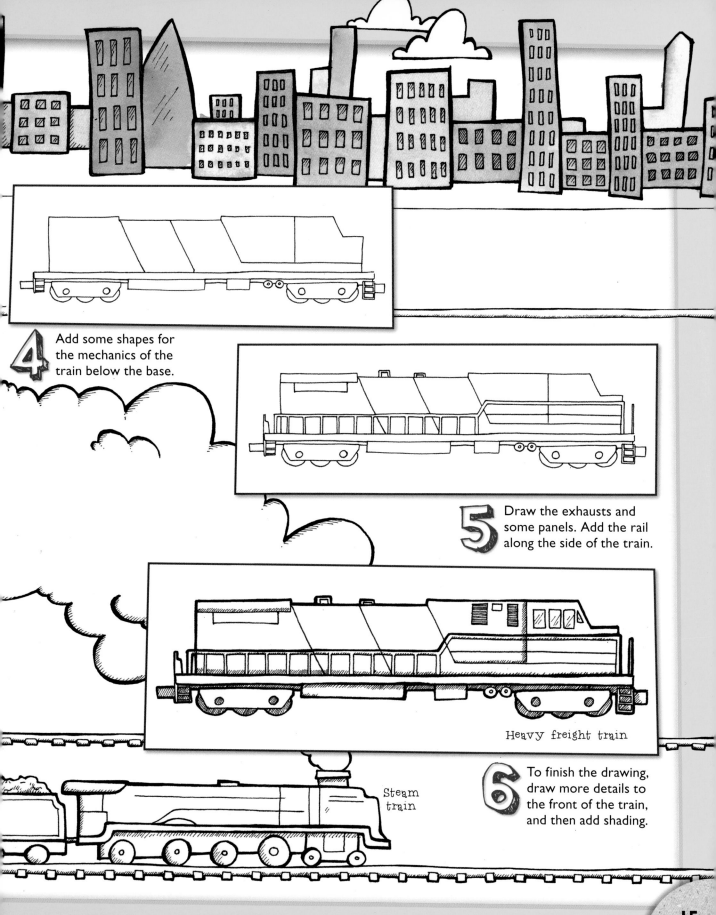

4 Add some shapes for the mechanics of the train below the base.

5 Draw the exhausts and some panels. Add the rail along the side of the train.

Heavy freight train

Steam train

6 To finish the drawing, draw more details to the front of the train, and then add shading.

How to Draw

Groovy Bikes

Riding bikes can be a fast way to travel. From pedal power to high-speed motorbikes, traveling on two wheels is always a lot of fun.

1 Start your drawing by sketching the main engine section of the bike.

2 Now add the two wheels to your bike. Draw in some pipes for the exhaust.

3 Draw the front fork, handle bars, seat, and then add the carburetor.

More to Draw

Bikes come in various shapes. Some have powerful engines, while others are powered by the rider.

4 Now you can start drawing details to the bike's wheels. Add spokes around the wheel.

5 Draw the mudguard and chain to the rear of the bike. Add a gearshift pedal and brake cable.

Chopper

6 To finish your drawing of this cool bike, go over the lines again and then add some shading.

Scooter

Sports bike

3-wheeled motorbike

Dirt bike

Penny farthing

Motorbike and sidecar

Rickshaw

Racing bicycle

Touring motorcycle

Rugged Racers

Monster trucks are customized pick-up trucks with huge wheels. They are used for racing, jumping, and doing cool tricks at truck shows.

1 Draw two large wheels. Add two circles in each wheel.

2 Join the wheels together with some lines. This will become the suspension.

3 Now you can add an outline for the truck's cab and bed.

4 Now add different support bars and struts to make this truck very strong and safe.

Monster truck

6 Finish your drawing by going over the lines again, and then add some shading.

5 Add details to the cab such as a window, steering wheel, and door. Decorate the tires of the truck.

How to Draw

Off-roaders

Off-road vehicles are designed to travel over rough or unusual terrain. These exciting vehicles don't let anything get in their way!

1 Draw two large wheels. Now add two circles inside each wheel.

2 Now draw an outline for the off-roader. Draw a line for each wheel arch.

3 Draw the doors and then the windows. Also add a panel for the roof and lid of the trunk.

4 Draw the bull bars at the front of the vehicle and the side step bars on the undercarriage.

All of these vehicles are designed to travel off road.
They can be added to drawings of rugged scenery.

Quad

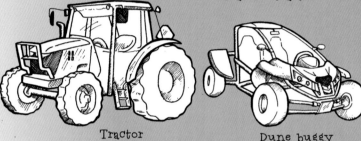
Crawler tractor

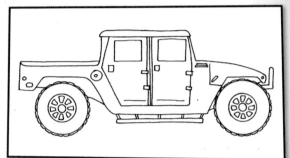

5 Add details for all the panels, hinges, air intakes, and fuel cap. Decorate the wheels and tires.

Tractor

Dune buggy

Off-road camper

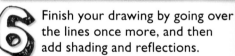
Hummer

6 Finish your drawing by going over the lines once more, and then add shading and reflections.

Amphibious car

Snow cat

Jeep

Pick-up truck

How to Draw

On the Water

People have used boats to travel on water for thousands of years. Some boats carry cargo, others are used for racing, and some are sailed just for fun.

1 Start your drawing with the hull of the power boat.

2 Now you can draw an outline above the hull for the cabin of the boat.

3 Add a top deck, and then draw a sweeping line from the front to the back of the boat.

Yacht

Cargo ship

Life raft

Fishing boat

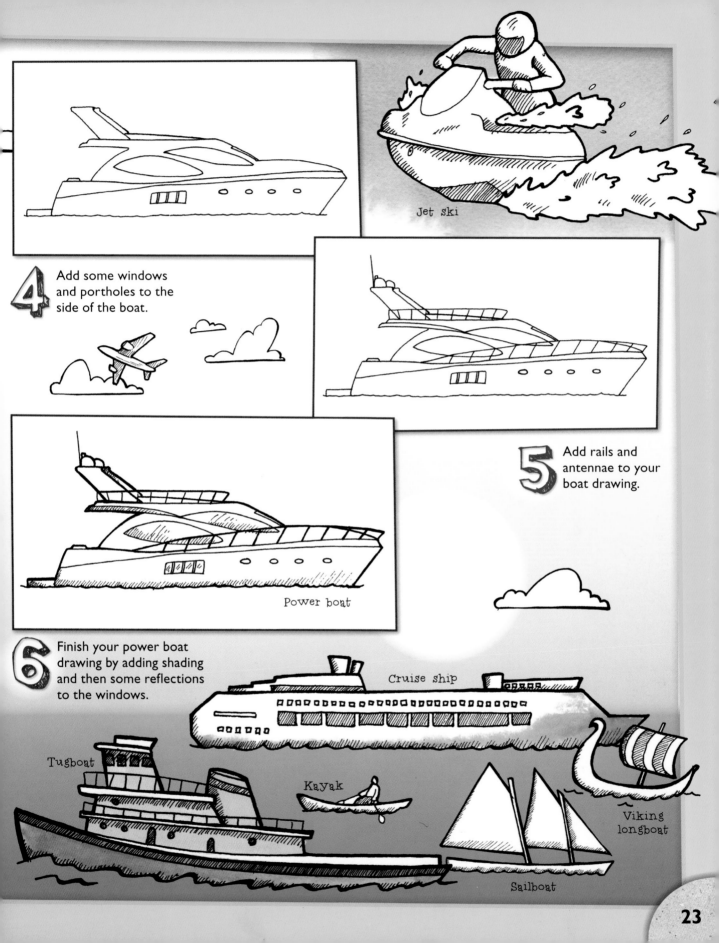

Jet ski

4 Add some windows and portholes to the side of the boat.

5 Add rails and antennae to your boat drawing.

Power boat

6 Finish your power boat drawing by adding shading and then some reflections to the windows.

Cruise ship

Tugboat

Kayak

Viking longboat

Sailboat

Underwater Explorers

Some vehicles are designed to travel under the water. These vehicles are used for research and for making repairs to underwater pipelines.

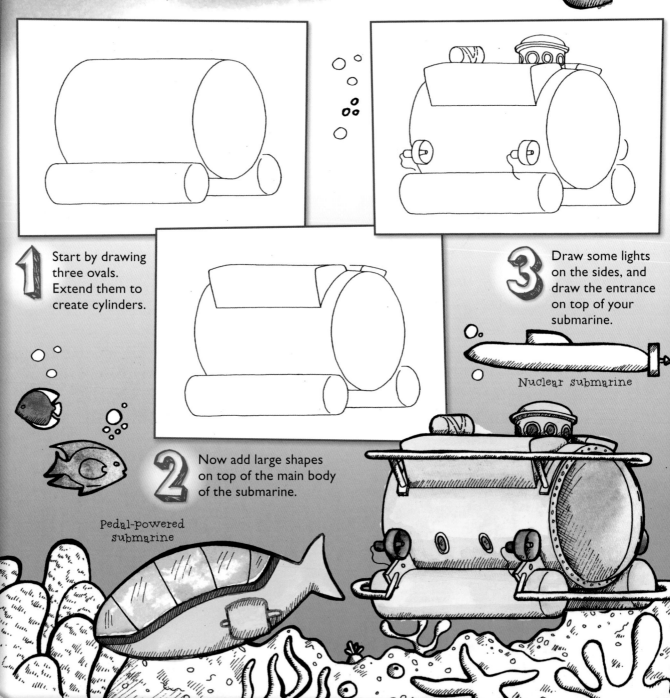

1 Start by drawing three ovals. Extend them to create cylinders.

2 Now add large shapes on top of the main body of the submarine.

3 Draw some lights on the sides, and draw the entrance on top of your submarine.

Nuclear submarine

Pedal-powered submarine

Remote control
underwater camera

4 You can now add both of the safety rails to your submarine.

One-man mini submarine

5 Draw two portholes onto the side of the submarine.

Underwater car

Deep-sea submarine

6 Finish your drawing by shading in areas and adding rivets.

How to Draw

In the Sky

There are many ways that we can fly through the air, from simple hang gliders and hot-air balloons to super-fast jet-propelled planes and helicopters.

Hang glider

Spy plane

1 Start your drawing with the outline of a helicopter.

2 Now draw a shape for the side panel on the helicopter and the engine cover on the tail.

3 Add a shape on the front of the helicopter. This is where the rotor transmission is housed.

4 You can now add two sets of rotary blades onto each end of the helicopter body.

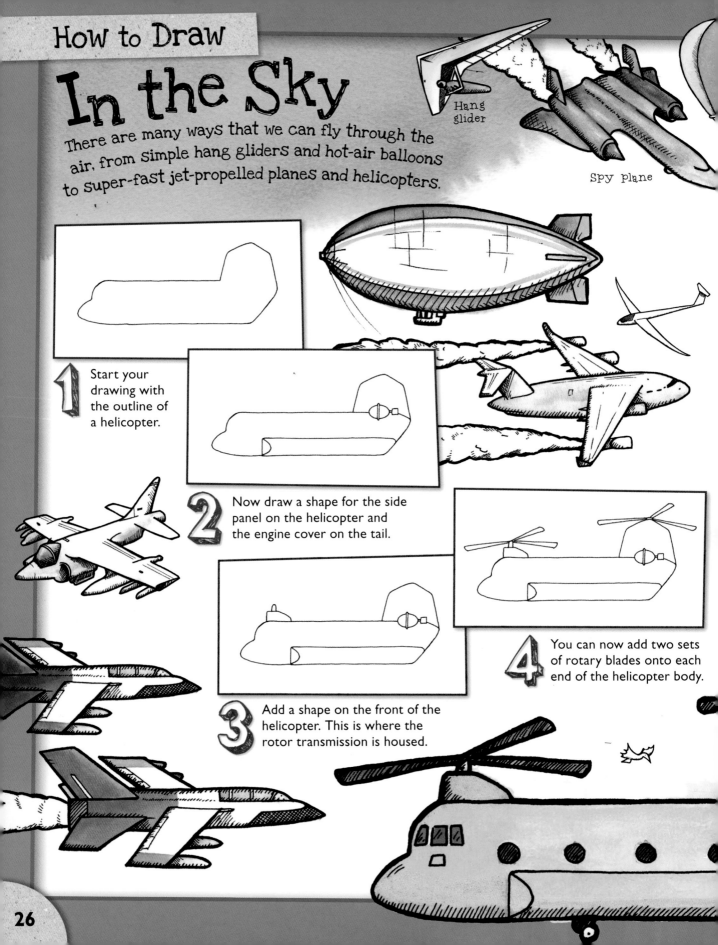

Try adding some of these suggestions to any of your drawings that show large areas of sky.

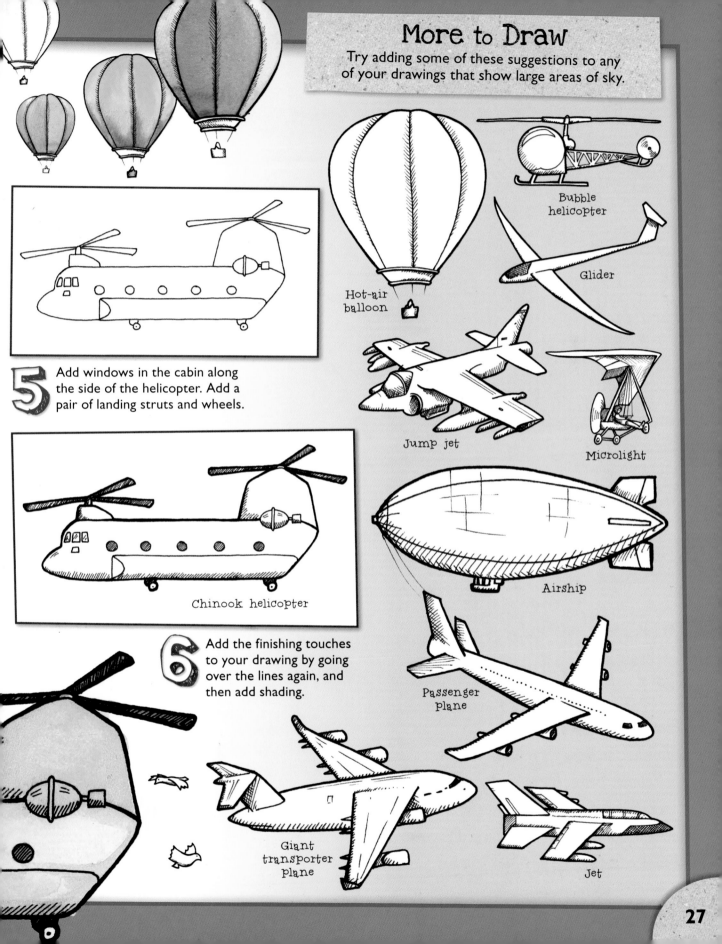

5 Add windows in the cabin along the side of the helicopter. Add a pair of landing struts and wheels.

Chinook helicopter

6 Add the finishing touches to your drawing by going over the lines again, and then add shading.

Hot-air balloon

Bubble helicopter

Glider

Jump jet

Microlight

Airship

Passenger plane

Giant transporter plane

Jet

How to Draw

Aerobatic Fliers

Aerobatic planes have been designed to show off the pilot's skills in flying. At some air shows, large groups of these planes will fly in perfect unison.

1 Start by drawing the nose. This is a cone inside a rectangle.

2 Now draw the outline of the plane. Leave gaps for the wing to be added.

3 Now you can draw the wings onto the side of the plane.

Triplane

Biplane

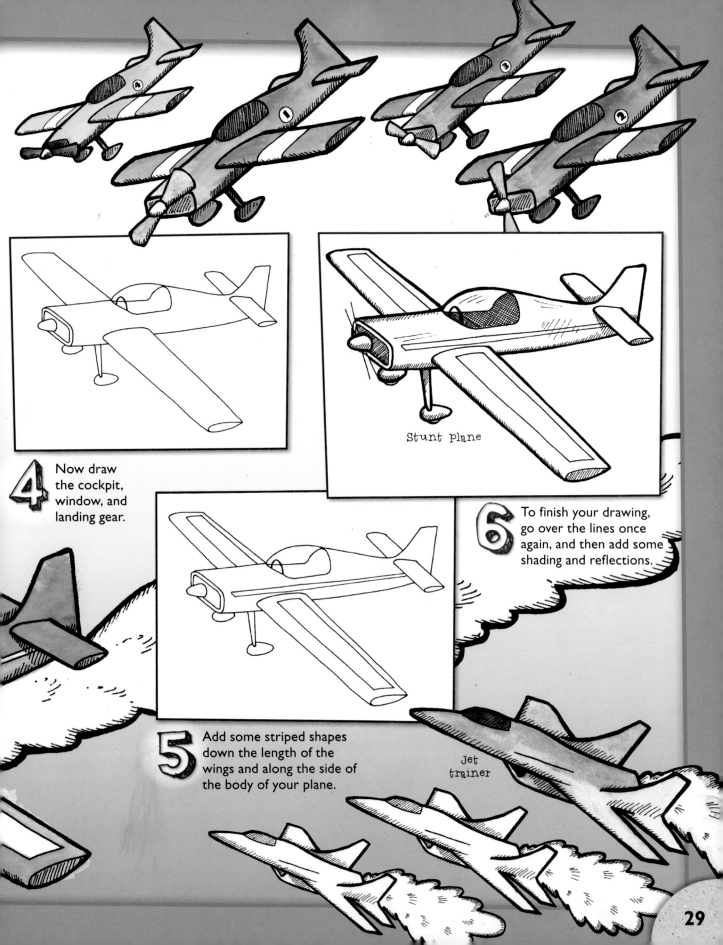

4 Now draw the cockpit, window, and landing gear.

Stunt plane

6 To finish your drawing, go over the lines once again, and then add some shading and reflections.

5 Add some striped shapes down the length of the wings and along the side of the body of your plane.

Jet trainer

How to Draw
Futuristic Travelers

Inventors are looking at new ways to improve our transport systems. We can only guess at how people may travel in the future.

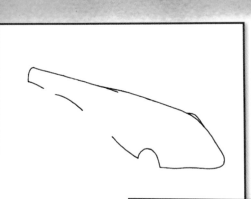

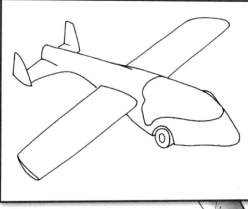

 Start with the skycar's outline. Leave gaps for the wings.

3 Draw a window around the cockpit and then add the wheel to your plane.

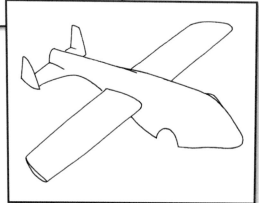

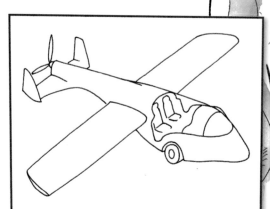

2 Add the wings to the side of the plane and to the rudder and stabilizer at the back.

4 Now draw some details in the cockpit and add a propeller to the back of the plane's tail.

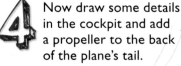

More to Draw
Here are some examples of future vehicles that
engineers and designers are currently working on.

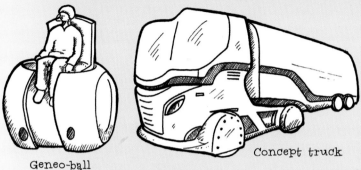

Geneo-ball

Concept truck

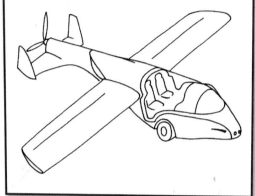

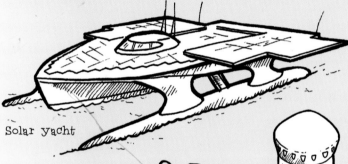

Solar yacht

5 Add detail to the body of the plane
with lines around the cockpit, nose,
and along the wings.

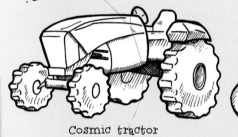

Cosmic tractor

Teleportation
device

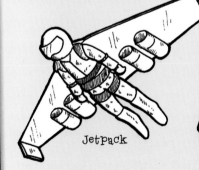

Jetpack

Electropositive car

Skycar

6 Finish your drawing by
shading some of the
areas to give a realistic
look to your plane.

Concept car

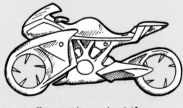

Concept motorbike

31

Vehicle Index

There are over one hundred different vehicles in this book. Practice your newfound drawing skills by adding some of them to your drawings.

3-wheeled motorbike	17
Airport fire engine	13
Airship	27
Ambulance	13
Amphibious car	21
Backhoe loader	8
Big rig	5
Biplane	28
Bubble helicopter	27
Bugatti Veyron SS	11
Bulldozer	9
Car transporter	5
Cargo ship	22
Chinook helicopter	27
Chopper	17
Concept car	31
Concept motorbike	31
Concept tractor	31
Concept truck	31
Concrete mixer	5
Crawler tractor	21
Cruise ship	23
Deep-sea submarine	25
Delivery truck	5
Dirt bike	17
Dragster	7
Dump truck	5
Dune buggy	21
Electropositive car	31
Endurance racer	7
Fire boat	13
Fire engine	13
Fire helicopter	13
Fire plane	13
Fishing boat	23
Forklift	9
Formula One car	7
Fuel tanker	5
Garbage truck	5
Geneo-ball	31
Giant dump truck	9
Giant excavator	9
Giant transporter plane	27
Glider	27
Grader	9
Gumpert Apollo	10
Hang glider	26
Heavy freight train	15
Hot-air balloon	27
Hummer	21
Jeep	21
Jet	27
Jet ski	23
Jet trainer	29
Jetpack	31
Jump jet	27
Kayak	23
Koenigsegg Agera R	10
Lamborghini Aventador LP700	11
Life raft	22
Lifeboat	13
Log transporter	5
Lowboy	5
McLaren F1	11
Microlight	27
Mini excavator	9
Mobile crane	9
Monster truck	19
Motorbike and sidecar	17
Nuclear submarine	24
Off-road camper	21
Off-road racer	7
One-man mini submarine	25
Passenger plane	27
Pedal-powered	
submarine	24
Penny farthing	17
Pick-up truck	21
Police car	13
Power boat	23
Quad	21
Racing bicycle	17
Rally car	7
Remote control underwater camera	25
Rickshaw	17
Road train	5
Roller	9
Sailboat	23
Saleen S7	11
Scooter	17
Skycar	31
Snow cat	21
Solar yacht	31
Speedway racer	7
Sports bike	17
Spy plane	26
Steam train	15
Stock car	7
Street racer	7
Stunt plane	29
Superkart	7
SWAT truck	13
Telehandler	9
Teleportation device	31
Touring motorcycle	17
Tractor	21
Tow truck	13
Triplane	28
Truck racer	7
Tugboat	22
Underwater car	25
Viking longboat	23
Yacht	22